Hide-and-Seek Kids

May Harte

Published in 2004 by The Rosen Publishing Group, Inc.
29 East 21st Street, New York, NY 10010

First Edition
Book Design: Kim Sonsky
Layout: Nick Sciacca
Photo Credits: All photos by Maura B. McConnell except p. 15 © Corbis

Harte, May
Hike-and-seek kids / May Harte.
p. cm. — (Hide-and-seek books)
Summary: Simple text challenges the reader to find
children hidden in photographs.
ISBN 1-4042-2816-0 (lib.)
1. Children—Juvenile literature   [1. Children
2. Picture puzzles]   I. Title   II. Series
                                                    2003—020118

305.23—dc21

Manufactured in the United States of America

The Rosen Publishing Group's
PowerStart Press™
New York

Where is the girl hiding?

Here she is ... under the bushes!

Where is the boy hiding?

Here he is ... in the ball pit!

Where is the girl hiding?

Here she is ...
behind the sandcastle!

Can you find someone hiding
in this picture?

Words to Remember

ball pit

bushes

sandcastle